Eras of Elegance

Fashionable Clothing 1850-1935
The Anna Lee Shetler Collection

Linda Phipps

Gold Horse Publishing
Annapolis, Maryland

To order additional copies:
Dollmasters, P.O. Box 2319, Annapolis, MD 21404
Telephone 410-224-4386   Fax 410-224-2515

Art Direction and Design: David W. Hirner
Photography: Robert Bartlett

Our thanks and appreciation to the following people for the loan of antique furniture
 and accessories to make the visual background beauty of this book possible:
Mark Russell-Woodward & Lothrop
Lois Scheminant-Annapolis Antique and Consignment Mall
Irene Repka-West Annapolis Antiques and Consignment Shop

ISBN 0-912-823-54-2
Printed in Hong Kong

Table of Contents

Chapter One   The End of a Century 1860-1899 6-11

Chapter Two   The Early Edwardian Era 1900-1907 12-27

Chapter Three Those Unmentionables 28-32

Chapter Four Late Edwardian to the Great War 1908-1919 33-53

Chapter Five A Lady's Accoutrements 54-70

Chapter Six   The Flapper and Depression Eras 1920-1935 71-89

Chapter Seven The Children's Closet 1850-1920 90-95

Chapter Eight Boots to Bonnets 96-109

Bibliography 110

Index 111

The Anna Lee Shetler Story

Who is Anna Lee Shetler? This lovely and refined lady is the caretaker of the fabulous collection of clothing gracing the following pages. This book is in honor to her as she passes on the care and preservation of these items to another generation of collectors. Here, in brief, is her story.

The Lee family history begins in the East. The family had settled in the tidewater regions of Maryland and later in the lush and fertile valleys and hills of West Virginia. As the area population increased, the family traversed to the Ohio territory and settled in the frontier. Ohio was a beautiful land and, again, crowding became a problem for this pioneering family. As the frontier moved farther west, so did the Lees. We begin our story with little Anna Belle Lee, the mother of Anna Lee Shetler.

The Lee family settled in the Oklahoma Territory where Anna Belle Lee spent her childhood and eventually grew up. At this time, the Indian tribes were being pushed aside to make room for all the land-hungry settlers. In 1893 Jordan Ray Williams was involved in the "Cherokee Strip" run for land in Oklahoma. Four years later, in 1897, this gentleman won the hand of the very fashionable Miss Anna Belle Lee. He served in the first four legislatures for Oklahoma from 1907 to 1913 as well as being president of the Oklahoma Press Association. Anna Belle was a strongly supportive wife who was also active in many women's groups. Young Anna Lee was born during this time in Lawton, Oklahoma.

The Williams family were also great pioneering spirits and could not long remain in one area. In the 1920's, they packed up their little family and set out for the final western frontier - California.

Being in the newspaper business, the family moved around frequently in the state to different areas. Anna Lee graduated from Beverly Hills High, spent one year at UCLA and went on to Chouinard's in Los Angeles to study fashion design. Her career was put on hold as she later married and raised a family in the outer Los Angeles area.

Her late husband, Mark Shetler, was a member of the Horseless Carriage Club which requires members to dress in vintage clothing for their auto tours. With her background in fashion, Anna Lee could not help but become passionate about the exquisite clothing of the early 1900's and began collecting complete costumes to wear. Her interest in her family history was also piqued at this time and she delved whole-heartedly into the joy of acquiring prime examples of clothing from the periods of history she was able to trace in her own family.

A few pieces from her original family collection blossomed into this collection of vintage treasures.

A Brief Fashion History

A privilege is to be granted a right, inferring that it is not the usual or common, but rather something to hold in reverence and awe, inspiring thankfulness that one is allowed to be a part of that privilege.

We have been accorded a privilege of history - to study a superb collection of clothing spanning the years of 1850-1935. This 75-year period provided some of the most phenomenal fashion changes as well as historical events which shaped the future of America as we know it today.

From cosseted and corseted to independent and free-swinging, one can observe how the role of women changed by the fashions of the era. By the 1880's, the size of a woman's waistline meant more than the size of her brain. Women rushed to squeeze themselves into steel bands and whalebone to try and achieve the ideal 17" waistline. Bustles were also worn to create a most unrealistic figure as well as a most uncomfortable one. The times were opulent as well as the clothing and continued so up to the turn of the century.

During the Edwardian era, the bustle disappeared but the corset stayed. A small waistline was still favored, although the figure became more of an hourglass with the "Pigeon breast" as the look of the time. The clothing took on a more romantic tendency - softly-flowing silks and batistes, an abundance of laces and trims. Clothing was still restrictive, dress bodices were still boned, sleeves became very tight as well as skirts as the years went by.

World War I, the Great War, arrived and women were forced to go outside the home to work in the absence of men. Necessity of movement dictated a change in fashion to enable women to survive. Hemlines went up. Waistlines went up and down. Clothing became simpler yet remained elegant.

After the war, the country was flushed with success, a sense of frivolity reigned and the Roaring Twenties was born. A time of celebration of youth, the silhouette of the age was pencil slim, straight and boyish. Hemlines rose dramatically and waistlines lowered to the hip. Clothing was loose and free-moving. Legs were bared at this time and fashion has not been able to cover them since.

Frivolity led to the glamour of the 1930's. The need for glamour to brighten the days of the Depression years became essential to the time. Bias-cut skirts and swirling georgettes with bright prints dominated the scene with classic, simplistic lines. This was more of a time of natural beauty of the figure without the artifice of restrictive undergarments or clothing.

Here we gently end our walk through fashion history. A freedom of movement began in the early part of the century. It is hard to believe it only took about twenty years to move from corsets to flapper dresses and how much that freedom of movement has affected women's clothes today. Each era was significant and each era had an individual elegance unequaled in any other time. It is hoped you will revere the clothing in these pages for their history and beauty as well as enjoy them as the Eras of Elegance.

5

Chapter One
The End of a Century 1860-1899

1. CINNAMON TAFFETA BALLGOWN
Two-piece silk taffeta gown consisting of seamed and darted bodice with plunging neckline decorated with three rows of taffeta ruffles and iridescent beads. Three-quarter length sleeves with pleated and ruffled edge with bow and vandyked embroidered lace undersleeves. Ruffle trim at armholes. Inset waistband with beaded applique and full overskirt with double ruffles extending from waistband around overskirt. Crocheted button-back closure with ruffled and beaded rosette at waist. Cartridge-pleated panelled skirt with train lined in cotton sateen. Net crinoline included. Circa 1870.

2. ALPACA WALKING SUIT
Milk-chocolate alpaca two-piece walking suit with princess-seamed jacket with embroidered panels over the front and back seams. Seamed waist, black gimp trim along the bodice front. Deep pleated ruffles at shoulder, embroidered cuff and hemline. Embroidered band along jacket hemline. Large embroidered bow at back waist. Front double bow closure with hook and eye. Black accordion-pleated silk plastron with black alencon lace collar and jabot. Panelled skirt with deep hem flounce, embroidered band and pleated ruffle trim along top of flounce, train. Cotton sateen lining and matching petticoat with dust ruffle. Circa 1865.

The End of a Century 1860-1899

3. AUBERGINE VELVET AND SATIN BALLGOWN

Aubergine-colored silk satin top with deeply plunging sweetheart neckline, elaborately embroidered and beaded black lace trim, intricate curved darts and blouson center-front panels. Eight-panel back with bias cut waistband. Slightly puffed three-quarter sleeves with bias-cut band, beaded medallion trim, pleated ruffle edging and black Chantilly lace undersleeves. Inner waist band signed "M.A. Connelly 7. East 16th St. 7, New York." Satin cummerbund with pleated back bow and V-shaped front. Elaborate pleated skirt of heavy, plum-colored cut velvet with center front satin band, satin draped mini-panniers with satin bow trim and crocheted and beaded tassels. Back of satin pleated into extended train. Pleated satin dust ruffle and pleated taffeta dust ruffle in front and organdy and lace-pleated dust ruffle around entire skirt. Bodice and skirt lined in silk taffeta. Skirt is also interlined with net and tartalane. Circa 1870.

4. BLACK SATIN AND LACE EVENING DRESS

Handstitched black silk satin basque with steel boning, seamed and fitted back with curved seamed and darted bodice. Black silk lace overlay with six ruched ruffles on front, black jet beaded trim along each ruffle and back bodice. White sateen plastron with black lace overlay. Leg o'mutton sleeves with lace sleeve ruffle and jet trim; hook and eye closure. Pleated satin neck collar with satin and lace side ruffles, hook and eye closure. Pleated satin ribbon waistband. Sateen lining. Gored satin skirt with pleated flounce, velvet "dust catcher" hem band, heavily gathered lace overlay with ruched waist trim. Cambric lining. Black silk taffeta petticoat with tucks and pintucking. Circa 1895.

5. KIDSKIN PUMPS
Black kidskin pumps with spool heels, high pointed tongue, large silk satin ribbon bows, silk grosgrain edging, leather soles. Circa 1880.

5A. SILK BASQUE
Printed silk basque with loose-fitting front, pink silk pleated plastron, lace ruffles down front, knife-pleated silk hem with lace overlay, black velvet ribbon trim and waist tie, fitted back with box and inverted pleat vent, pleated lace trim on mandarin-type collar, fitted sleeves with lace edge ruffle and velvet bow, original waist tape. Circa 1900.

6. SILK ORGANZA AFTERNOON DRESS
Lavender striped silk organza two-piece dress is bias cut. The top has a blouson effect with four rows of ruching along yoke. Standup collar with six rows of ruching and velvet trim. Double-puffed upper sleeves with ruching around each puff with straight lower sleeve with ruched and velvet-trimmed edge. Front hook and eye closure. Gored bias-cut skirt with five rows of ruching around top of skirt and hip area. Deep hem flounce with slight train. Wide printed silk ribbon sash with bouffant bow. Circa 1890.

7. WHITE SATIN BEADED SHOES
White satin pumps with four straps, iridescent beaded design on vamp and straps, four blue glass shoe buttons, kid lined, spool heels, leather soles. Manufactured by "C.H. Baker, Los Angeles." Circa 1880.

8. VOILE AFTERNOON DRESS
Pink and white striped with black printed voile two-piece dress with pleated blouson top, high standup collar covered with pink silk ribbon trimmed with two bands of black velvet ribbon with bow at back, two velvet-trimmed ruffles around bodice and back, unusual side front opening, large pink ribbon bows and ruffle down left bodice side. Puff at upper sleeve with ruffle on top and bottom, straight long tight sleeve with two rows of velvet trimmed ruching down the sleeve, pink bow trim. Embroidered lace edge ruffle. Panelled front skirt with gathered back. Six rows of velvet-trimmed ruffles set in rounded diagonal pattern around skirt with train. Pink silk cummerbund with bow at back. Batiste lining. Circa 1890.

8A. FLORAL TRIMMED STRAW BONNET
Straw bonnet with upturned and shaped brim has black velvet band around edge, chenille and floral bud trim, pink silk organza ribbon gathered around crown, black velvet bows, and large cloth roses with more chenille and floral bud trim. Circa 1890.

9. PINK KID MULTI-STRAP SHOES
Pale pink kidskin pump with four-strap fastening, two cutouts on vamp, all trimmed in silver studs and tiny silver beads, black shoebuttons, leather sole, modified spool heel, lined in white kid. Circa 1880.

10. VELVET AND LACE BLOUSE WITH FRENCH LABEL
Unusual blouse made of strips of black velvet ribbon and inset rows of guipure lace over a silk chiffon underblouse. Stand-up collar of velvet and lace. Puffed upper sleeve in Juliet-style with straight lower sleeve with hook and eye closure; cuff lined with satin ribbon. Attached and pleated velvet cummerbund. Cotton-lined and boned bodice. Inner waist tape is stamped "Marie Longerey, Robes & Manteaux, 74 Rue Taithbout, Paris." Circa 1890.

11. HANDMADE BATTENBURG LACE BLOUSE
Soft ivory blouse of handmade Battenburg lace in Gibson style with stand-up collar, long sleeves with pouf at top, snug waist with pouched front and V-shaped waistband. All lace is handstitched together to form the elaborate floral pattern. Circa 1890.

12. ECRU SATIN EVENING COAT
Three-quarter length silk coat of ecru satin in A-shape with wide three-quarter length sleeves trimmed with two rows of gimp, rounded neckline with gimp trim and double capelet collar trimmed in gimp. Three handmade frog closures of string and fine rope with beaded tassels. Heavily-padded interlining, lined in moire. Circa 1890.

13. WOOL JACQUARD CAPE
Very fine wool jacquard cape with princess-seamed back, seamless front, heavy, thick fringe of various widths and types of silk ribbons around entire cape and neck. Fringed front hook and eye closings. Heavy quilted silk lining of cotton batting. Circa 1880.

14. BATTENBURG LACE JACKET
Slim-fitting jacket of handmade Battenburg lace has fitted sleeves, leaf design around collar, split vent at center back, one frog closure at front with tassels, cutaway style front, lace all handstitched. Circa 1880.

15. BATTENBURG LACE COAT
Knee-length coat of handmade Battenburg lace, open front, seamless, slightly flared. Wide, straight long sleeves. Circa 1890.

The End of a Century 1860-1899

Chapter Two

The Early Edwardian Era 1900-1907

16. SILK AND VELVET TEA GOWN

Two-piece costume of pastel printed silk on pale green background. Basque top has high, stand-up Point de Gaze lace collar with Valenciennes lace ruffle, pleated organza plastron decorated with fine galloon lace with ribbon embroidery, a softly gathered bodice fastens over plastron with hook and eye. Shoulders have pale green epaulets with pink velvet-covered button trim. Bodice edge and sleeves trimmed with galloon lace with ribbon embroidery. Boned under-bodice of pleated print silk with two rows of velvet bias trim and a velvet frontispiece trimmed with four pink velvet buttons. The upper under-bodice is of lace-trimmed cotton. A flared silk cape sleeve with velvet epaulet trimmed with four buttons covers a sheer pouf sleeve of pleated silk organza trimmed with embroidered galloon lace gathering into a lower sleeve of three rows of valenciennes lace. The bottom of the sleeve is trimmed with a knotted and twisted green velvet band. The skirt is constructed with partially stitched-down pleats around the waist falling into a soft train. Around the bottom of the skirt are four medallions of pleated organza and embroidered lace. Circa 1905.

17. SILK TEA GOWN

Palest gray-green dupioni silk bodice has a pintucked capelet-collar and pleated bodice, high standup collar with pink velvet edging and embroidered floral trim. A double row of ruched organza topped by the embroidered trim surrounds the capelet collar. Back bodice is pleated. Large pouffed and pleated upper sleeve extends into tight, straight pintucked and velvet-trimmed lower sleeve with ribbon-trimmed and velvet-edged cuff. Sleeve bottom is decorated with ruched organza and embroidered trim. Ruched and pleated sash. Partially stitched-down box-pleated skirt with train. Circa 1905.

18. SILK BROCADE WEDDING GOWN
Ivory silk brocade two-piece gown with palest pink printed roses in background. Sheer appliqued lace yoke over pouched silk pintucked bodice and back. Stand-up lace collar, full pouffed Spanish-style sleeve with seven tiers of valenciennes lace ending in a short straight lace cuff. Unique lace-trimmed silk oversleeve of rectangular band attached at shoulder and hanging loose over sleeve. Appliqued lace on oversleeve and bodice. Back hook and eye closure. Hip-stitched pleated silk skirt with train. Unlined. Circa 1905.

19. SILK BROCADE WEDDING GOWN
Heavy oyster silk brocade gown of bodice and separate skirt. Diagonal pintucked yoke of bobbinet with brocade pouched bodice, the brocade extending up over the shoulders like bretelles. The edge is done in French knots. Tiny stand-up collar trimmed in French knots and edged with handmade Point de Gaze lace. Handmade Point de Gaze appliques decorate the bodice and back. Aqua silk ribbon with beaded and crocheted tassels intricately knotted in front bodice. Upper puffed sleeve of bobbinet over chiffon undersleeves. Lower sleeve of diagonal pintucked bobbinet with lace appliques trimmed with brocade rosettes and bows and French knots on the cuff edged in pleated and fagoted chiffon. Attached sash of gathered silk trimmed in back with six rosettes. Panelled skirt with an inverted-pleat train. Underskirt of cotton with double row of pinked-edge silk ruffles. Hem edged in velvet. Circa 1905.

20. SATIN WEDDING SLIPPERS
Nearly mint ivory silk satin wedding slippers with pointed toes, soft kidskin lining and bow trim. Modified spool heels, leather soles. Manufactured by "J & J Slater, Broadway, NY." Circa 1915.

21. SILK TAFFETA BALLGOWN

Boned bodice of black embroidered silk taffeta with inverted V-shaped back, front pleated panels and stand-up collar of rose printed on ivory silk faille trimmed with black Chantilly lace and black lace applique, sequin and beaded design outlined in metallic and black cord trim, front hook and eye closure, wide Chantilly lace ruffle from waist extending over shoulder. Pouffed elbow-length sleeve is pleated into a gathered bias cut band and edged with wide silk ruffle lined with faille, lower undersleeves of Chantilly lace. Sateen lining, inner waist tape, pleated bodice bottom forms a point in front. The front panel of the skirt is the silk faille in inverted pleats. Self-fabric box-pleated trimmed hem. A row of wide Chantilly lace drapes from waist to hem on either side. The side and back skirt of embroidered taffeta has a row of box-pleated black taffeta trim around skirt and train. The train extends over five feet along the floor with hook to attach to waist for walking. Inner-lining of lightweight taffeta with scalloped and pinked dust ruffles. Circa 1900.

22. LACE AND BEADED BALLGOWN

Black satin and taffeta bodice overlaid by accordion-pleated silk chiffon. Deep rounded neckline with tulle modesty piece. Tulle faux jacket front and back with intricate sequin and bead design and handmade lace appliques. A sequined and corded leaf trim is attached on bodice neckline. Short sleeves of loose poufs of pleated chiffon with trimmed cuffs, bretelles of the trimmed tulle. Back hook and eye closure, velvet waistband with sequined and embroidered trim. Inner waist tape labelled "Schaefer Importer, Rochester, N.Y." Panelled skirt with tulle overskirt with intricately beaded and sequined design with handmade lace. Tiny chiffon hem ruffle on overskirt, long train, chiffon pleated ruffle and taffeta dust ruffle with box-pleated trim on underskirt. Circa 1905.

23. SILK BROCADE BOLERO SUIT

Short bolero jacket of peacock silk satin yoke and black brocade diagonally pleated from arm. Front darts, fitted back with diagonal ribbon trim and handmade lace ruffle. Standup collar of jet and bugle beads and velvet ribbon trim. Wide pouffed short sleeves with ribbon cuff trimmed with handmade lace ruffle. Blouse of black handmade lace with daisy braid design, leg o'mutton-style sleeves, stand-up collar, underlining of peacock silk satin with changeable silk taffeta lining. Intricately-corded and beaded belt of peacock silk. Panelled skirt of brocade with two wide rows of black silk ribbon trim and handmade lace, short train, lined in brown cotton sateen and interlined with crinoline. Circa 1900.

23A. MATCHING HAT

Black plush veiled bonnet molded over buckram frame is trimmed with black velvet ribbon, peacock silk and black silk poufs and a large pair of black bird wings. Velvet underbrim, silk lining. Circa 1900.

24. LACE SHIRTWAIST

Ecru shirtwaist of delicate lace with net front and back inserts and high stand-up collar edged in ecru silk satin. Both front and back are trimmed with Duchess lace appliques. The bodice has two tucks over each shoulder and gathered waist with front pouching, long straight sleeves with crocheted trim on cuffs. Ecru silk lining. Circa 1890.

24A. CUT VELVET SKIRT

Deep brown cut velvet over apricot background panelled skirt has train and back gathers. Lined in cotton sateen with a buckram hem lining and velvet dust catcher. Brown velvet sash with ornate gold buckle and hook and eye closure. Circa 1890.

25. FUR AND OSTRICH BONNET

Wired bonnet with wide front upturned brim has soft beaver fur crown and underbrim, ombre velvet leaf trim at back and peach, apricot and brown ostrich feathers as decoration. Upper brim and inner crown of brown silk. Circa 1890.

26. SHORT FUR JACKET

Short jacket of soft beaver fur matches above hat. Jacket has wide lapels and collar, long straight sleeves with slight gathers at shoulder, crocheted loop and button closures, fitted princess back, two inner pockets of chamois leather, brown silk lining. Label from "Wm H. Miller & Co. Furs, Detroit, MI." Circa 1890.

27. LADIES FUR MUFF

Large beaver muff to match jacket and hat has black velvet ruffles at openings black, silk lining and black and brown carrying cord. Circa 1890.

28. WOOL WALKING SUIT

Boned jacket of fine black wool with plain yoke has diagonally tucked bodice with rows of fagoting and silk ribbon, flower and leaf braid yoke trim, inverted "V" pattern of tucks, fagoting and ribbon on jacket back with two hanging tabs trimmed with crocheted buttons. High stand-up collar of ribbon and trim with tabs and lace neck ruffle. Slightly-gathered sleeve at shoulder extending into wide pouch at bottom with tabs and fagoted cuffs. Black silk satin waistband. Silk and cotton sateen lining. Gored skirt with plain front panel, fagoting and ribbon trim on sides, back and hem, front and back tabs, box pleated back with French knot design at back hook and eye and snap closing, velvet dust catcher, black linen underslip with hem ruffle. Circa 1903.

29. BEADED VELVET BONNET

Small wired bonnet of black and navy velvet with upturned front brim which has been beaded and embroidered. Crown covered with jet beading, burgundy silk ribbons and rosette trim at back, curled burgundy ostrich feather trim. Circa 1900.

30. LACE AND VELVET BALLGOWN

Boned bodice of handmade lace lined in heavy ecru satin, black velvet bands of sequin and jet floral designs over front of bodice, delicate jet and bead fringe design at neckline, deeply pouffed elbow-length georgette and lace sleeves with handkerchief-style edge and bead-trimmed cuff. Pleated georgette center front panel, inner waist tape with manufacturer "Julia de Pomeroy CSW Dressmaker 189 Conduit Street 88." The skirt is lined in heavy satin panelled with train. Overskirt of lace panels with vertical velvet beaded bands around the skirt and around the hem and train, organdy and lace dust ruffles. Separate black velvet beaded belt. Circa 1905.

31. BEADED PURSE

Square-shaped purse of leaf-type design in fine beading of black and silver, vandyked beaded bottom, ornate silver frame, double fine chain handle, flower-shaped button to open purse, silk lining. Circa 1900.

The Early Edwardian Era 1900-1907

32. MAN'S EVENING SUIT WITH TAILS AND EXTRA TROUSERS

Man's cutaway evening jacket of fine black wool, darts in front, fitted and seamed back with long tails trimmed with two black silk-covered buttons, straight sleeves with faux double button closure, silk faille lapels, faux button front, silk lining. Black wool trousers with button fly front, black silk ribbon trim down each side seam, two hidden side seam pockets, two welted back pockets, suspender buttons. Also pair of wool black and gray striped trousers with back cinch strap, button fly front, on seam pockets, welted back pockets, suspender buttons. Circa 1900.

33. COLLAPSIBLE OPERA HAT

Black silk faille opera hat with collapsible mechanism, faille silk ribbon and bow trim, black silk lining, label "Extra Quality/Dieu Et Mon Droit/Regent St/London".

34. LADIES AFTERNOON DRESS

Rose-beige silk dress with tiny woven dot design has boned bodice, pleated net yoke with bias fabric and French knot trim, handmade lace yoke trim with Chinese knots, high lace collar, silk bretelles over sleeves of silk three-tiered upper sleeve and lower sleeve of pleated and trimmed net, silk lining. Semi-circular skirt with cutout lace trim on front and sides, gathered section at skirt bottom, three rows of tucks around hem, eight rows of shirring on sides of skirt, looped self-fabric trim on side and back seams, train. Circa 1905.

35. FUR WRAP

Luxurious brown sable wrap six feet long with two rows of tail and back leg tassels, brocade silk lining. Circa 1900.

36. FUR MUFF

Large deep brown mink muff with brown silk lining, ruched and gathered, brown carrying cord with crocheted ball at end. Circa 1900.

36A. SILK PARASOL

31" Length. Beige silk satin with silk lace trim gold and maroon silk lining, varnished natural wood handle. Mechanism intact.

37. PANNE VELVET EVENING GOWN

Rust panne velvet evening dress with embroidered velvet bodice and georgette modesty piece with corded ruching, embroidered velvet bretelles edged in Irish crochet over one-piece ombre georgette sleeves and side panels with corded ruching and embroidered velvet cuffs, all silk lined. Skirt front panel has handmade Irish crochet, hand and machine embroidery and fagoting. Vandyked embroidered hem, deep "V" back neckline, georgette-ruched back, long embroidered pleated train with Irish crochet, lined in heavy satin. Circa 1900.

38. DUPIONI LADIES SUIT

Mocha dupioni silk jacket with embroidered silk bodice panels, long pleated side front and back panels with soutache braid trim, capelet over straight three-quarter sleeves with embroidered panels over folded cuffs, six velvet buttons on front, collar of dupioni with accent trims of rust velvet and cream satin triangles, back center panel of fan-pleated silk, frog closures for side panels. Stitch-pleated skirt with ten button trim, soutache braid on lower front panel, button trim at back waist and back skirt sides, silk panel between side buttons. Circa 1905.

The Early Edwardian Era 1900-1907

39. COTTON SHIRTWAIST AND SKIRT
White dotted Swiss shirtwaist with tucked inset, center front and back, lace insertion, delicate handmade lace yoke and collar, slightly-gathered sleeves with same lace decoration, button back closure. Full gathered dotted Swiss skirt with two wide flounces of handmade lace ruffles with beading and pink satin ribbon trim. Cotton underlining with dust ruffle. Circa 1905.

40. LINEN AFTERNOON DRESS
Petal-pink linen blouse with embroidered wheat design on front, back and sleeves, Point de Gaze lace-covered stand-up collar, jabot and cuffs. Hook and eye and snap closure. Long saddle-panelled skirt with flat felled seams, wheat embroidery around waist and on each panel. Circa 1900.

40A. ROSE-TRIMMED STRAW HAT
Natural straw bonnet with upturned brim and cloth pink and fuchsia cabbage roses garland, palest pink chiffon intertwined with flowers, black silk lining. Circa 1900.

40B. RAFFIA HAT WITH OSTRICH PLUME
Gray woven raffia and horsehair turban with two embroidered horsehair plumes lined in pink silk over upturned brim, gathered woven crown, rhinestone and metal buckle on front, gray velvet underbrim, molded buckram frame, silk lining. Circa 1905.

41. GARDEN PARTY DRESS
White batiste dress with tucked Broderie Anglaise lace yoke, intricate insertion work on bodice and tucked skirt, bishop sleeves with pintucking and insertion work, Broderie Anglaise cuffs, jewel neckline, coral pink silk moire sash with large bow and back floral trim. Circa 1905.

42. WIDE-BRIMMED STRAW HAT
Natural straw hat with wide flat brim, cloth spring flower wreath on bed of aqua tulle and ribbons. White silk lining. Circa 1905.

43. WHITEWEAR DRESS
White cotton lawn dress with squared neckline of insertion lace, tucked and gathered bodice with center panel of lace, pouching at waist, two rows of insertion at waist, slight pouffed sleeve with tight tucked lower sleeve, insertion and vandyked ends, tucked back bodice. Lightly gathered skirt has two front vertical tucks, two rows of insertion above deep hem flounce with tucking. Circa 1900.

44. DOTTED SWISS VISITING DRESS
Two-piece dress of dotted Swiss with black dots on ecru background in different patterns alternating with net. Low-cut front with pleated and pouched center front panel. Black Chantilly lace trim around neckline, bodice front and back yoke. Chantilly lace dickey-front over sheer lawn with standup collar. Bishop sleeves with lace trim, velvet ribbon cuff trimmed with bows. Hip-stitch pleated skirt with Chantilly trim and two tiers of tiny knife-pleated ruffles. Circa 1905.

45. FLORAL BEADED RETICULE
Drawstring bag of black beads with center colorful garden flowers, row of pink roses at bottom, black crocheted top, black drawstring cord, beaded tassel at bottom, satin lined. Circa 1900.

46. SHEER LACE EVENING WAIST
Black Chantilly lace blouse with deep neckline, sheer upper bodice, tulle underbodice with Chantilly ruffles, silk satin pleated waistband with bow, lace peplum, sheer straight elbow-length sleeves with cutouts and fluted lace ends. Boned satin interlining, lace-up front, all handstitched. Circa 1900.

46A. BATTENBURG LACE SKIRT
Long flared skirt of handmade Battenburg lace with Point d'Esprit panel inserts, crocheted lace waist band, slight train. Unlined. Circa 1905.

47. CROCHETED LACE SHIRTWAIST
Ecru crocheted lace blouse has center front panel, two tucks over each shoulder, narrow elbow-length sleeves with tucks, pouched front, standup collar, Irish crochet on collar, neck, front and back yoke and sleeves, silk lining. Circa 1905.

48. BEIGE BEADED RETICULE
Drawstring handbag of crystal beads with rose pattern on crocheted beige background, floral pattern around bottom of taupe and gold beading, green and gold beaded tassel. Circa 1900.

49. SILK SHANTUNG COAT
Collarless beige coat of shantung with one long embroidered panel of flowers which extends around coat from front to back to front. Two front patch pockets with embroidery, straight sleeves with embroidered semicircular cuffs, silk lining and plush interlining, hook and eye closures. Circa 1900.

50. IRISH CROCHET COAT
Three-quarter length flared coat of white Irish crochet of raised daisies and leaves. Finer crochet around edges, neckline, and hem. Slightly flared elbow-length sleeves, crocheted button closure. Circa 1900.

51. IRISH CROCHET DRESS COAT
Flared dress-length ecru coat of Irish crochet of raised floral pattern is sewn in panels with godet inserts, collarless, sleeves gather into straight high cuff with two rows of satin trim, satin lining. Circa 1900.

52. LADIES BEADED COLLAR
Black jet beaded collar over black faille and ecru satin. Heavy collar extends to waist, rounded lined upper collar. Large black satin bows at neck, black accordion-pleated silk ruffle with ecru pinked and pleated under-ruffle, front hook and eye closure, back silk underarm ribbons, front ribbon sash. Circa 1890.

53. PLEATED NECK RUFF
Black silk accordion pleated neck ruff of 6 layers of ruffles, long pleated silk ties. Circa 1880.

54. LADIES BEADED COLLAR
Black faille collar to extend to waist in front and back has intricate floral beading design, bugle bead fringe, stand-up collar, silk waist tie. Circa 1880.

54A. BOX OF MEN'S COLLARS
Maroon cardboard box of men's fabric collars contains eight starched men's white collars in new condition. Original tissue and printed paper cover. Outside label reads "Creston/Trade Ide Mark 15 1/4/Geo. P. Ide & Co. Makers/Troy, N.Y. USA 2 3/8 - 1 3/4". Circa 1905.

The Early Edwardian Era 1900-1907

Chapter Three
Those Unmentionables

55. SATEEN MORNING DRESS OR WRAPPER
Black cotton sateen print dress of bamboo and floral design has pintucked yoke and beige velvet ribbon and lace trim, pintucking on sleeves, cuffs trimmed in ribbon and lace, black lace capelet ruffles on sleeves which extend to back waist, cuff ruffles, princess-seamed back with pleated train, black satin sash pleated and sewn in diagonal manner in back, crocheted rosette trim, stand-up collar of ribbon and lace. Front hook and eye closure. Circa 1900.

56. LADIES MORNING COAT
White muslin coat with Swiss embroidered yoke, front panel and cuffs. Tucked and gathered front, back gathered under embroidered yoke, long bishop sleeves with button cuffs. Button and buttonhole front closure. Circa 1880.

57. LADIES NIGHTGOWN AND SPLIT DRAWERS
White batiste cotton nightgown with front and back yokes of patterned Valenciennes lace insertion and Swiss embroidery. Elbow-length split angel sleeves with lace insertion, beading with ribbon and mechlin lace ruffles. Rounded drawstring neckline of mechlin lace ruffle and ribbon-threaded beading. Featherstitched hemline. Split drawers with lace insertion, pintucking, beading and ruffles to match gown.
Circa 1890.

58. MORNING SACQUE
Short loose-fitting muslin jacket with rows of tiny tucks, shirred fabric and more tucks in right angle patterns, neck and sleeve ruffles, straight sleeve with tucked and shirred pattern, godet inserts for fullness at sides, semi-fitted princess-seamed back with tucks and shirring.
Circa 1900.

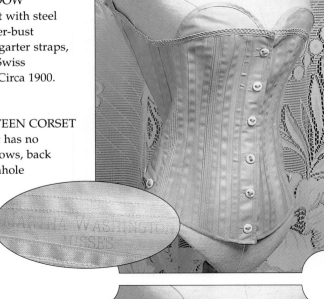

59. BLACK MERRY WIDOW
Black cotton sateen corset with steel boning, back lacing, under-bust shirring, extended front, garter straps, white twill lining, black Swiss embroidery trim at top. Circa 1900.

60. CAMBRIC AND SATEEN CORSET
Pearl gray cambric corset has no boning, closely stitched rows, back lacing, button and buttonhole front closure, modesty bust covers, cambric straps, metal garter straps. Stamped label "Martha Washington Misses." Circa 1900.

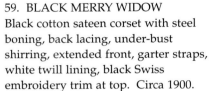

61. BLACK SATEEN CORSET
Ladies corset of black cotton sateen is boned, bias-cut sateen trim with flat-felled seams, back lacing, lace and ribbon trimmed top edge, unlined, hook and eye closure, original stamp "M.G. & Co." Original tag "M.G. & Co./405/Size 23." Circa 1900.

62. BLACK SATEEN CORSET
Black sateen boned corset is lined with cambric, waist tape, black lace and ribbon trim on top and bottom, hook and eye closure, back lacing, original stamped label "R & G No. 93." Circa 1900.

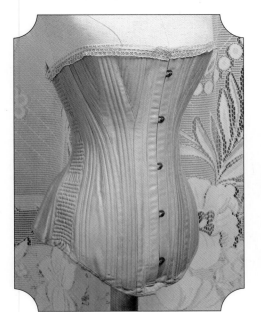

63. TAN SATEEN CORSET
Long tan cotton sateen corset has boning, side elastic shirring, back lacing, hook and eye closure, stitched and formed bust cover, lace top trim. Circa 1910.

64. BLACK SATEEN CORSET
Long black cotton sateen corset is boned and lined in coutil with back lacing, decorative stitching, hook and eye closure, black Swiss embroidery top trim, stitched and formed bust cover. Original stamped label "Style 222/'Kid Fitting'". Circa 1900.

65. LONG PRINCESS SLIP
Full-length slip of white batiste has princess seams, rounded neckline, lace ruffle trim on armholes, deep tucked hem ruffle with insertion and lace edging, embroidered trim along top hem ruffle seam, button and buttonhole front closing. Circa 1908.

66. LONG PRINCESS SLIP
Full-length slip of white batiste has Swiss eyelet-embroidered top with beading, rounded drawstring neckline with Valenciennes lace trim around neck and armholes, eyelet front panel, deep eyelet hem ruffle with tucking and beading, plain under-ruffle, back button and buttonhole closure. Circa 1910.

67. COUTIL CORSET
Long pale pink corset of cotton coutil has boning, back lacing, two elastic inserts at hip, hook and eye closure, elastic garters, lace and embroidered braid trim at top, original stamped label from Warner's. Circa 1910.

68. LADIES PETTICOATS
Lot of three white cotton petticoats each with cotton lace trimmings; one has a v-shaped waistband and lace-edged V-shaped insets, one has self-turned waistband, tuck and ribbon-trimmed lace ruffle, one has rows of insertion and separately-applied waistband and pleated back. Two have under ruffles. Circa 1905.

69. LADIES PETTICOATS
Lot of two muslin and one batiste petticoats. One has wide separately-aplied waistband, deep back gathers, separate banded back hem flounce, rows of alternating wide and narrow tucks, Swiss-embroidered hem flounce, one with self-turned waistband, rows of pintucking and five rows of lace insertion with scalloped lace edge on the flounce, one with separately-applied waistband, Swiss embroidered insertion, rows of pintucking alternating with insertion and deep hem flounce with scalloped edge Swiss embroidery. All have under ruffles.

70. LADIES PETTICOATS
Lot of three white cotton petticoats. One has rows of pintucking, Schiffli insertion band and Schiffli-embroidered hem ruffle, one has rows of tucking alternating with lace insertion and Schiffli-emboidered hem flounce and separately-applied waistband, one has rows of pintucking alternating with rows of Swiss embroidered insertion of snow flowers and Swiss-embroidered hem flounce and taped waistband and back pleating.

Chapter Four
Late Edwardian to the Great War

71. GOLD WOOL EMBROIDERED DRESS

Pale gold wool one-piece dress has sheer Alencon lace yoke and high stand-up collar with lace capelets over short sleeves. The bodice has pintucking and self-fabric embroidered cutout medallion trim across bodice, back, waist, sleeves and hem. Slightly gathered waist, straight skirt with plain front panel with tuck on either side, hook and eye closure down back side panel, gold satin sash with bow and tassels, long cotton underslip with wool hem to create tiered look. Circa 1910.

71A. WHITE BEAVER HAT

Large white beaver hat has upturned brim on one side, sage green satin ribbon and flower decoration, green velvet leaves, large sage ostrich feather, silk lining. Circa 1910.

72. BEADED PURSE

Small purse with crystal and green bead design, bead fringe, silver filigree frame with ornate closure, silver chain handle, crepe lining. Circa 1915.

73. GOLD MESH BAG

Rectangular-shaped bag of fine gold mesh with vandyked bottom and ball trim, plain gold frame, large link chain handle. Circa 1910.

74. SATIN AND VELVET EVENING GOWN
Nutmeg brown silk satin one-piece gown with diagonally pleated front and back bodice, velvet inset in front and back with jeweled bead braid trim. Guipure lace upper bodice and stand-up collar with satin trim, velvet bands on edges of bodice, pleated upper sleeve with velvet braid-trimmed cuff over guipure lace, three-quarter length lower sleeve with satin trim. Long skirt with plain front panel with knife pleated front side panels. Satin pleated sash with back rosette, wide satin band around skirt side and back, jeweled trim on back bodice, side front hook and eye closure. Circa 1910.

75. PHEASANT HAT
Brown molded beaver felt wide-brimmed hat has coiled braid trim and three quarters of pheasant body including tail feathers to trim top of hat, jeweled medallion at front of hat, silk lining. Circa 1910.

76. IRIDESCENT BEADED BAG
Brown crocheted purse with iridescent brown/gold beads in vertical patterns, beaded fringe, square brass frame with embossed and filigree design, crepe flowered lining with soft braid trim. Circa 1910.

77. SILK BEADED EVENING GOWN

Silk satin high-waisted dress of midnight blue with sheer black silk overdress, deep square neckline, beaded net inset, beaded trim around neckline, front bodice, sleeves and skirt, large black jet beaded pattern on bodice, beaded fringe on bodice front and sleeves, overskirt caught up pannier-style in front with embroidered and beaded flowers, shirring on black silk oversleeve, undersleeve is short, beaded and net covered with crenalated edge. Diagonally gathered back on overdress over netted and beaded underdress with beaded trim around neck and down back seam, jet and bead trim at waist. Overskirt is shorter and of varying lengths to drape over underskirt. Circa 1910.

78. SILVER BEADED BAG

Small narrow crocheted purse of gray cotton covered with silver beadwork and fringe with ornate frame and clasp, beaded bottom tassel, silver link chain handle, brocade lining. Circa 1900.

79. SILVER MESH PURSE

Small purse of fine silver mesh with rounded embossed frame, vandyked and fringed bottom, ornate silver chain mesh handle. Circa 1900.

80. TAFFETA AND LACE GOWN
High-waisted gown of rose printed taffeta silk with embroidered lace draping over georgette bodice, lace and velvet rosette on front with rhinestone buckle, short sleeves of georgette covered with lace and rose velvet ribbon trim, georgette and lace front panel with lace tiers on side front and long rose velvet bands decorated with rhinestone buckles, corded silk waist band, side front opening, sheer lace back bodice, slight train. Circa 1910.

81. NET AFTERNOON DRESS
One-piece dress of fine ecru net with gathered bodice and lace appliques, lace insertion inset and straight collar. Tucked elbow-length sleeves with insertion and lace ruffles. Bias-cut skirt with insertion and tucks, china silk underdress, wide ecru moire silk sash that ties in back. Circa 1910.

82. ROSE-TRIMMED BEADED EVENING DRESS

Pink silk satin gown has square neckline, straight design, net overskirt with iridescent sequin and silver round and bugle bead trim. Scalloped net draping on either side of dress, cloth roses on shoulder and sprinkled on overdress. Tiny net decorated shoulder overlays, gathered high-waisted back, pink cloth roses trim back neckline, silk underdress has beading design in front and back, row of cloth roses around the hem, inner waist tape with original stamp "Robes/G. Stelljies/1318 Madison Ave./New York," hook and eye back closure. Circa 1910.

83. IRISH CROCHET DRESS
Simple dress of ecru Irish crochet. Overdress has gathered bodice, flared skirt over gathered pale aqua silk crepe underskirt which extends below the overdress, short sleeves, bodice and sleeves lined in aqua silk. Various vertical and horizontal patterns of crochet. Aqua and pink silk satin sash with double rose trim. Circa 1910.

84. LINGERIE DRESS
White cotton batiste princess-style dress is covered with elaborate array of guipure, valenciennes, Swiss embroidery, cutwork, filet lace and pintucking, horizontal tucks around skirt, standup collar, short sleeves with lace trim, back closure of lingerie buttons and thread loops and hook and eye closure, china silk lining of palest blue. Circa 1908.

85. SEA-GREEN SILK WIDE-BRIMMED BIRD HAT
Wide flat-brimmed hat of molded buckram and wiring covered in pale sea green silk with ruched silk band, wired and gathered underbrim, cloth spring flower and sea green velvet ribbon and bird head and wings spread over hat, silk lining. Circa 1910.

       Chapter Four

86. BATISTE DAY DRESS
White cotton batiste dress has guipure lace yoke, rounded neckline with alternating vertical rows of guipure and insertion with two rows of tucking on bodice and skirt with lace and guipure insertion and one-piece sleeves with guipure lace down the top of the sleeve and Valenciennes ruffle. Skirt has wide and narrow tucking alternating with lace insertion and lace insertion waistband. Circa 1915.

87. WHITEWEAR DAY DRESS
White cotton batiste dress has empire waist, squared neck of Valenciennes lace, pintucked bodice and back with insets of pintucking and embroidered batiste with rows of Schiffli embroidery, fagoting and crocheted ball trim. Softly gathered skirt alternates rows of pintucking with Schiffli embroidery and fagoting. Scalloped and embroidered hem. Inset sleeves of pintucking and embroidery with crocheted ball trim at edges. The back has crocheted ball trim in a diagonal line along embroidered panels. Button and loop closure. Circa 1910.

88. PINK AND WHITE LINEN WALKING DRESS

Two-piece linen dress of white and pink linen is decorated with Irish crochet on bodice, stand-up collar, undersleeve section and upper sleeve and cuff. Pink silk pleated yoke and upper sleeve lining, white linen faux jacket front and lower straight sleeves with pink linen bodice and waistband. Pink linen panelled skirt with side back tuck pleats and inverted pleats at back closure. Irish crochet trim with white linen hem. Circa 1915.

89. WHITE COTTON DAY DRESS

Heavy cotton poplin dress has gathered bodice with tucks over shoulder, high waisted, crocheted lace neckline, front and back panels over bodice and skirt with lace trim, short sleeves with lace inset and cotton band trim, vertical tucks on skirt front and back panels. Circa 1910.

90. RAW SILK DRESS
Beige raw silk sleeveless dress has front panel of embroidered lace, soutache and crochet trim. High waist, gathered bodice with tucked shoulders, square neckline, tassel trim at waist, front panel with two long stitched-down pleats on either side, low squared back with side opening, four stitched-down pleats on skirt, tucked and trimmed back bodice. Circa 1908.

91. YOUNG MISS WHITEWEAR DRESS
White cotton batiste dress of Swiss eyelet embroidery for young teen with yoke of pintucking and insertion. Elbow-length sleeves with scalloped edges, gathered waist, scalloped hem, back hook and eye closure. Circa 1915.

92. EMBROIDERED NET OVERDRESS
Long ecru net dress with embroidered floral design has surplice-type bodice and back with black velvet trim and ruffle, circular skirt with several rows of tucks and tiers of vertical pintucking, twill-taped waist, back hook and eye closure. Circa 1910.

93. APPLIQUED LACE OVERDRESS
Ecru net with handmade lace appliques on entire dress. Bias cut skirt with train, lace overpanel on front, net tab on back bodice which is high waisted, remains of silk underdress bodice, short sleeves gathered up on sides with lace oversleeve, satin trim. Circa 1910.

94. GRAY FLANNEL SUIT
Long princess-style wool flannel jacket has tab decoration, shawl collar, back belt, long tabs on back with button decoration, welted buttonholes, silk lining, straight sleeves with pleated shoulders. Straight panelled skirt with four inverted bottom pleats, unlined. Back zipper closing. Circa 1915.

95. LADIES STRAW BOATER
Woven raffia straw hat has flat brim, black veil covering hat, wide grosgrain ribbon and bow trim. Grosgrain silk inner band lining. Circa 1912.

96. PARISIAN TURBAN
Black silk satin turban with molded buckram and wire brim, black peacock feathers and jet medallion and silk fluted ribbon trim. Ecru silk lining with original label "Andree Delmond/16ter Avenue bosquet/Paris." Circa 1910.

97. BLACK AND WHITE HI-TOP SHOES
Black and white kidskin leather high-topped shoes with perforated hole decoration, wooden spool heels, leather soles, grommets and laces. Circa 1910.

Andrée Delmond
16ter Avenue Bosquet
PARIS

98. VELVET SUIT
Deep navy velvet two-piece suit with long fitted jacket, small collar and lapels, open front with heavy black braid trim and large crocheted buttons, full bishop sleeves with cuff and three faux buttons, princess seamed, split back with deep pleats. Original label "Castberg/Chicago." Full skirt with stitched-down pleats, train, black silk taffeta underskirt with dust ruffle. Circa 1908.

98A. VELVET AND OSTRICH HAT
Black velvet molded hat with short brim on left side extending to wide brim on right, black jet trim, velvet bow, ivory and navy ostrich feathers curled around hat, silk lining. Circa 1910.

99. MOIRE BEADED PURSE
Small black moire bag with beaded floral design, embossed brass squared frame with push-button clasp, double chain handle. Original frail silk lining with attached change purse. Circa 1910.

100. EMBROIDERED COLLAR SUIT
Pine green wool flannel suit below hip-length jacket has embroidered black velvet collar, wide lapels, two welted buttonholes and covered buttons, cutaway bottom, pieced back with pleats and button trim, straight sleeves with button and faux tab closure, silk lining, original label "Meekins, Packard & Wheat/Springfield, Mass". Skirt has straight back with deep horizontal tuck, front has curved tucks down front, pleat and button trim at bottom, unlined. Circa 1915.

101. GOLD BEADED BAG
Pouch-shaped bag of gold crochet with gold bead pattern, fringe, bottom tassel, original silk lining, decorative mesh chain handle. Circa 1910.

102. GABARDINE THREE-PIECE SUIT
Below hip length ivory wool gabardine jacket has princess seaming, button and tab decoration, narrow lapels, three-button closure, straight sleeves with button and tabs, fitted back with button and tabs, two split vents. Gored skirt with button and tab decoration on front, two godet insets on back and deep inverted pleat at back, straight waistband. Silk blouse with net overlay containing soutache braid, guipure, lace embroidery and pintucking. Pintucked modified leg o'mutton sleeves, satin trimming on yoke. Pleated back bodice with guipure trim. Circa 1914.

102A. RAFFIA STRAW HAT
Turban-style hat of natural raffia straw with wired brim, large peach silk bow, rust velvet leaves and white cloth flowers, cotton underlining. Circa 1910.

103. LARGE BEADED BAG
Gold, silver, and crystal beaded bag of fine beads, fringed bottom, floral embossed frame, gold chain handle, push button clasp, jacquard silk lining. Circa 1900.

104. WHITE SUEDE HI-TOP SHOES
White suede high-topped shoes with suede spool heels, leather soles, perforated decorations, punched holes and lacing. Circa 1910.

105. DUPIONI SILK SUIT

Collarless below hip-length jacket of ecru dupioni silk has embroidered silk shaped front panels with slightly gathered bust, tab around neckline with inset lace, cutaway front, embroidered three-quarter sleeves gathered at elbow into split cuff with lace inset. Plain back bodice with V-shaped lace inset yoke, large tab with button trim and embroidery at bottom, lined. Skirt is gored with stitched-down pleats. Circa 1911.

106. AMETHYST-ENCRUSTED BROCADE PURSE

Small rounded purse of purple, red, gold and gray brocade with corded seams, original lavender silk lining, ornate embossed silver scalloped frame with seven glass amethysts on each side, double silver chain handle, tiny pine cone snap clasp. Circa 1900.

107. TINY FRENCH PEARL AND SEQUIN FABRIC BAG

Small bag of heavy woven fabric with metallic threads of rose and green, braid along seams, floral design of tiny gold beads, gold sequin leaves, pearl-trimmed white velvet flowers and rhinestones. Square embossed gold frame with cut out sections, vandyking with rhinestone insets, row of pearls, snap clasp, oblong chain link handle, original faille lining with label "Made in France for Milnor, Inc." Circa 1910.

108. AQUA COAT AND MATCHING HAT
Aqua wool broadcloth flared coat with trapunto stitched yoke, square-edged lapels with handstitched floral trim of silk, soutache, braid and embroidery and trimmed with forest velvet and guipure lace ruffles. Cutaway-style front with two large embossed brass buttons, long puff sleeves with shoulder shirring and wide trimmed cuffs, fronts of coat lined with guipure lace to simulate picot-style edging. Fitted back with upside-down V-shaped trapunto-stitched yoke, ivory silk lining. Wired flat-crowned hat of aqua wool with large flat crown covered with cherry-patterned lace, wide-shaped brim with handmade trim, ivory silk pleated band ribbon, ivory silk lining with ruching around edges and trim on raised front. Circa 1908.

109. FOX-TRIMMED SILK COAT
Blue ombre silk satin coat with metallic gold embroidered leaf design, low shoulders, white arctic fox trim around shawl collar and cuffs, peach silk crepe padded lining. Circa 1920.

110. BROCHE WRAP EVENING COAT
Peach silk broche full-length wrap coat with charcoal velvet design, pleated front, separate yoke with button and loop closure, hip-length frog closure, charcoal velvet semi-detachable oblong collar with corded gathering in front and four corded ties with petal ends, long wide sleeves with charcoal velvet cuffs with corded trim, peach lining, original label "James McCreery Co./New York." Circa 1913.

111. BROCHE DRAPED EVENING COAT
Ecru silk broche full-length draped coat has below-hip button and loop closure, long draped collar with metallic gold braid and tassels, ecru silk lining, long straight sleeves with ecru silk cuffs and gold metallic braid. Circa 1913.

112. SILK PONGEE DUSTER
Beige unlined lightweight silk pongee duster coat has bias-band covered princess seaming with two patch pockets, brass buttons and buttonhole closure. Fitted princess back also has bias- covered seams, long straight sleeves with turned-up cuffs. Circa 1908.

113. BLOUSON CAPELET
Unusual bittersweet silk velvet capelet is gathered at neck and back seam and draped to form pouching to keep the elbows nestled inside. Long velvet neck sash, coral silk lining. Circa 1930.

114. IRISH CROCHETED BLOUSE
White cotton Irish crocheted blouse and shaped yoke, stand-up collar, fitted sleeves with hook and eye closure, extended center front, back yoke, hook and eye closure. Circa 1910.

115. BOLERO FRONT LACE JACKET
Ecru Guipure lace jacket with bolero front extending into longer fitted back, embroidered net band around front and hem edges ending at center back. Circa 1910.

116. PLUSH PURSE
Black plush purse is rounded with pointed bottom with two cotton tassels, embossed silver-plated brass frame with snap clasp, silver chain handle, original beige silk lining with braided trim. Circa 1900.

117. BEADED SILK PURSE WITH GEM TRIM
Unlined black silk bag has silver bead and black bugle bead design on front, silk tassel at bottom, silver double-hinged frame that opens from the center into square, filigree trim on frame with faux glass pink tourmaline gems on front, plain back, snap clasp, silver chain handle. Circa 1900.

118. SMALL BLACK MISER BAG
Crocheted black miser bag purse with cut steel beadwork, fringe and tassel, two crocheted rings and silver ring closures. Circa 1890.

119. LARGE GOLD MISER BAG
Gold crocheted miser bag with carrying handle, gold and silver cut steel beadwork, beaded tassel with silk fringe, beige cord with gold embossed ring closure, silk crepe lining. Circa 1890.

120. GOLD AND LAVENDER BEADED BAG
Square-shaped purse of extra fine cut steel beading of lavender, gold and silver in geometric patterns, beaded vandyke fringe in honeycomb pattern. Square silver embossed leaf design frame has floral push-button clasp, embossed chain handle, pink silk lining with braid trim.

121. PINK BEADED PURSE
Crocheted purse of pink crystal beading with swag and fringed design. Square gold floral embossed frame with snap clasp closure, fine embossed chain handle, silk lining with metallic braid trim. Circa 1910.

122. MESH VANITY BAG
Armor mesh purse with embossed Chinese pagoda top which opens with small cabochon sapphire clasp, mirror in top with imprint on mirror rim "Armor Mesh", gathered mesh bottom with gold filigree-headed mesh tassel, chain link handle. Similar to vanity bags produced by Evans and Whiting and Davis. Circa 1922.

123. MESH BAG
Enameled silver armor mesh bag by Whiting and Davis with vandyked bottom, silver-plated ornate openwork frame, snap knob clasp, original tag inside "Whiting and Davis Co./Mesh Bags", twisted chain handle. Circa 1910.

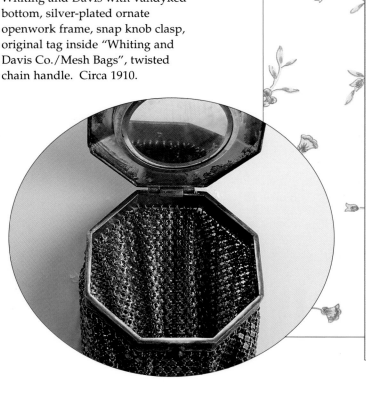

124. FRENCH CUT STEEL BEADED PURSE
Square-shaped purse of fine multi-colored cut steel beads depicting the Bridge of Sighs in Venice, Italy with a gondolier poling the river. Beaded fringe, embossed and filigreed square frame inset with faux jewels, snap knob clasp, silver chain handle, original "made in France" label on lining. Circa 1900.

125. FRINGED BEADED EVENING BAG
Closely beaded bag of black in triangular shape with rounded embossed silver frame and heavily fringed bottom, embossed chain handle, lined, snap knob clasp. Circa 1920.

126. DIAMOND-SHAPED BEADED BAG
Triangular-shaped bag of gold knit cotton decorated with ivory beading in rows, loops and fringe, ornate embossed and filigreed diamond-shaped frame, embossed chain handle, snap knob clasp, silk lining with braid trim. Circa 1920.

127. GINGER DIAMOND-SHAPED BEADED BAG
Ginger-colored cotton knit bag densely beaded in rows with thick bottom fringe. Ornate gold and silver embossed frame with cutwork and cherub design, snap knob clasp, beaded handle. Circa 1920.

128. OPALESCENT BEADED BAG
Diamond-shaped bag of white cotton knit with opalescent crystal beading and fringe. Embossed and filigreed triangular frame with snap knob clasp, chain handle, silk lining. Circa 1920.

129. LOT OF JEWELED PURSE FRAMES
Four brass and one silver ornate cutwork frames of which two have handles, all have assorted encrusted faux jewels, three have snap knob clasps, one has snap jewel clasp and one has knob clasp. Circa 1910.

130. TWO DRAWSTRING RETICULES
One peau de soie silk drawstring bag has embroidered roses and embroidered scalloped edges, silk lining, bone ring closures with satin ribbon, silk lining. Second bag is simple white cotton crochet with grograin drawstring. Circa 1925.

131. CROCHETED RETICULES
Three purses of raised crochetwork are all lined and have drawstring handles and crocheted ball fringe, one white, one ecru and one ginger-colored. Circa 1910.

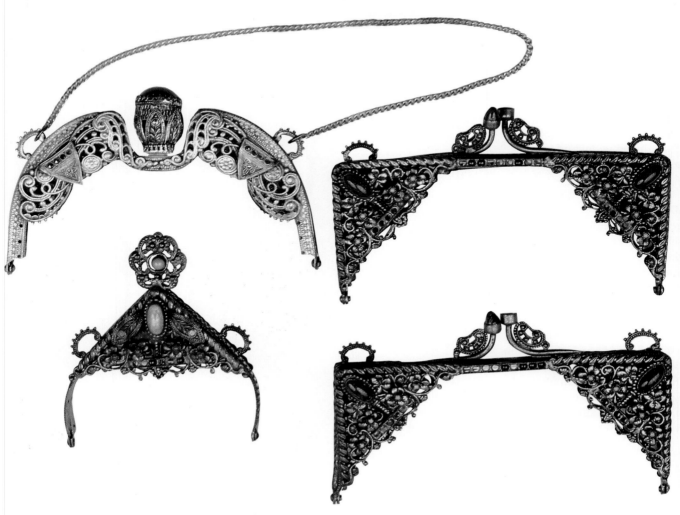

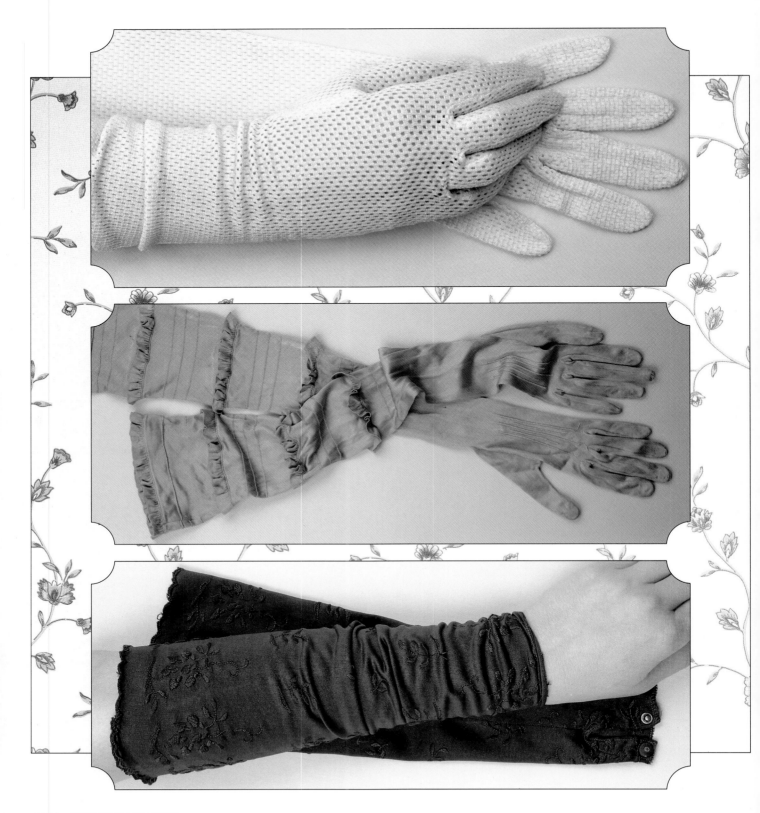

132A. SILK KNIT GLOVES
Ivory knit silk dress gloves in below elbow-length have tiny rectangular pattern, one seam. Circa 1910.

132B. EVENING GLOVES
Pale gray knitted silk shoulder-length gloves with snap closures, decorative stitching on back of hand, four tiers of ruffles with three rows of decorative stitching between tiers. Circa 1910.

132C. EMBROIDERED MITTS
Nutmeg brown knitted silk embroidered mitts have picot edging at wrist, scalloped top edge, one-snap closure, elbow length. Circa 1900.

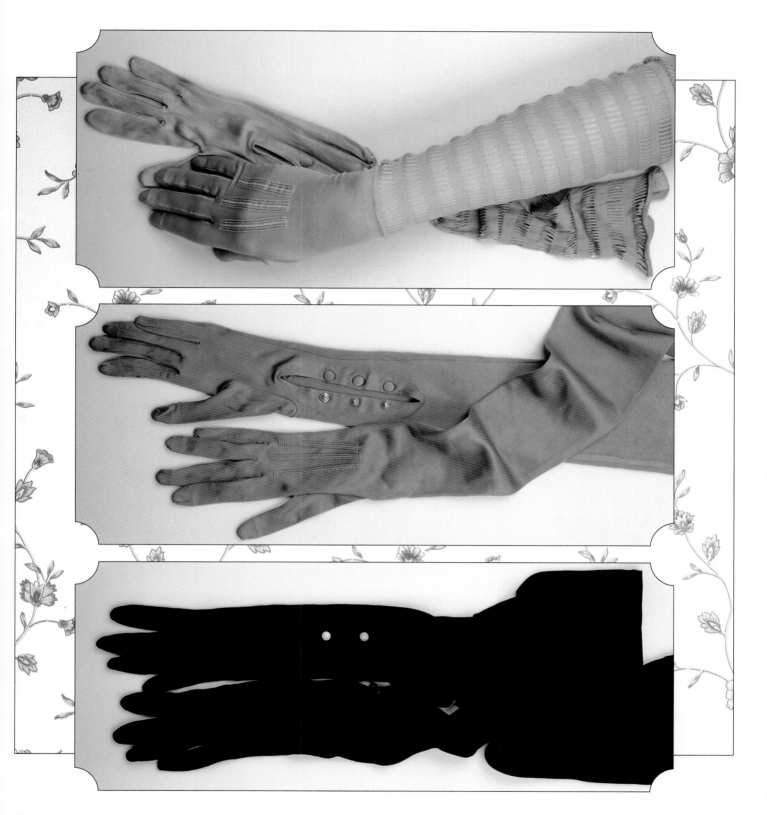

133A. OPERA GLOVES
Pearl gray knitted silk gloves in opera length have decorative stitching on back of hand, two-snap closure, unusual lacy openwork from wrist up. Original labels "Van Raalte 6 1/2" and "Made of Silk in U.S.A. 6 1/2". Circa 1910.

133B. OPERA GLOVES
Burnished gold knitted silk gloves in opera length have three-button closure, decorative stitching on back of hand. Circa 1910.

133C. SILK EVENING GLOVES
Black knitted silk evening gloves in shoulder length have plain fronts, two gray mother-of-pearl buttons and buttonhole closure. Circa 1910.

134A. BRACELET-LENGTH GLOVES
Cinnamon bracelet-length knitted silk gloves with decorative stitching on back of hand, two-snap closure, original stamp "'Kayser' Four * Silk/6/Pat'd Jun 28'98/Made in USA." Circa 1898.

134B. BRACELET-LENGTH GLOVES
Identical to previous lot, except in camel and identification on snap, not a stamp. Circa 1898.

134C. WRIST GLOVES
Identical to previous two lots except in black and in shorter length with one-snap closure. Circa 1898.

134D. SHORT CROCHETED GLOVES
Short white cotton crocheted gloves with raised loop pattern on back of hand. Circa 1900.

134E. CROCHETED BRACELET-LENGTH GLOVES
White cotton crocheted gloves in gauntlet-style bracelet length, crocheted one-button closure. Circa 1900.

134F. CROCHETED BRACELET-LENGTH GLOVES
Ecru cotton crocheted gloves in slightly flared style with diamond pattern in bracelet length. Circa 1900.

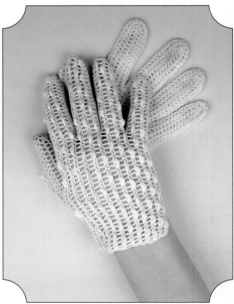

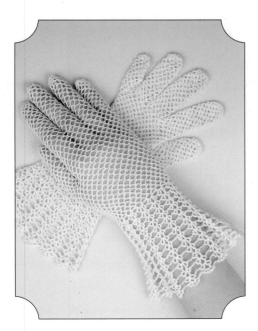

135. PARASOL WITH TORTOISE EAGLE CLAW HANDLE
30" length. Black Chantilly lace over gold silk cover, ivory silk lining. Upper handle of bamboo, lower handle of carved tortoise shell in well-detailed shape of eagle claw holding ball in curved talon. Mechanism intact.

136. PARASOL WITH MOTHER-OF-PEARL AND GOLD HANDLE
37" length. Black silk twill cover with lace insertion, top ruffle of net and Chantilly Lace, edge ruffle of Chantilly lace and net with black beaded trim. Wooden upper handle with lower handle of embossed gold metal alternating with two sections of carved mother-of-pearl, gold metal embossed knob with initials "LK" on end, pompom tassel. Mechanism intact.

137. SCHIFFLI EMBROIDERED PARASOL
36" length. Ecru cotton cover with black Schiffli embroidery, top ruffle. Wooden upper handle with lower handle left raw and knotty with large knot at end, cotton cord with tassel, button loop closure. Extra cotton parasol cover included. Mechanism intact.

138. SILK AND LACE PARASOL WITH BAMBOO HANDLE
36" length. Ivory silk satin cover with two tiers of fine lace and top lace and net ruffle. Bamboo handle with curved end, gold metal embossed decoration on handle. Mechanism intact.

139. WOOD-HANDLED PARASOL
41 1/2" length. White muslin cover with embroidered designs over pale blue silk ruched lining with silk edge ruffle. Shirred ruffle at top. Carved wooden handle with knob end. Mechanism intact.

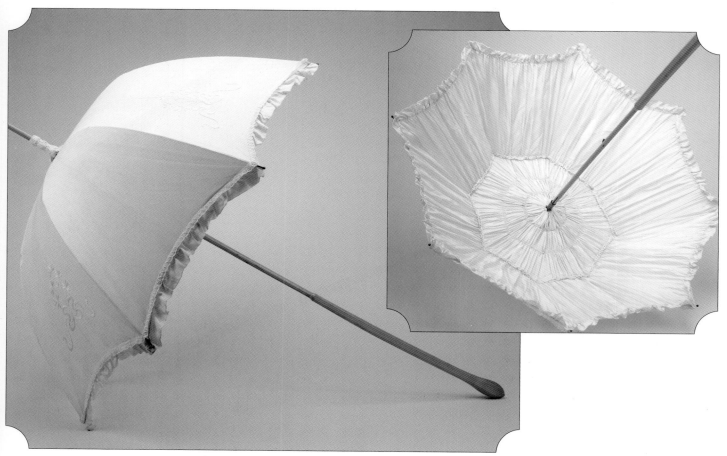

140. COLLAPSIBLE LACE PARASOL
24 1/2" length. Sheer black net cover with beaded lace appliques, crocheted lace ruffle, bone upper handle with carved bone curved lower handle. Metal stay. Mechanism intact.

141. COLLAPSIBLE SILK PARASOL
27" length. Black faille silk parasol with raw scalloped edges, black silk lining, wooden black painted handle with carved leaf design and curved bottom handle. Metal stay for stiffening. Mechanism intact.

142. EMBROIDERED FRINGED SHAWL

Ivory three-piece silk crepe capelet shawl with embroidery in floral pattern, honeycomb and tasseled silk fringe along front and around hem, frogged corded ties with triple end tassels. Large crocheted button and tassel decorations on back. Circa 1900.

142A. OSTRICH FAN

12" H. Celluloid handle and struts in tortoise look with rose red trimmed ostrich feathers. Early 20th century.

142B. OSTRICH FAN

25" H. Tortoise-look celluloid frame contains brown/black curled ostrich plumes. Early 20th century.

143. SILK SHAWL
Black silk lace oblong
shawl with picoted and
scalloped edging.
Approximately
108" x 32".
Circa 1890.

**144. CHANTILLY LACE
SHAWL**
Large triangular-shaped
shawl of black Chantilly
lace. Appears to be early
machine made.
Approximately 108"
across, 54" center
measurement.
Circa 1860.

**145. BATTENBURG
CAPELET**
Ivory bolero-style capelet
of handmade Battenburg
lace with stitched
trumpet sleeves, ivory
silk velvet edging,
organza and blue velvet-
trimmed front bodice
flowers, sheer silk
organza lining.
Circa 1900.

146. LACE SURPLICE JACKET
Ecru guipure lace surplice-style jacket has daisy pattern with crocheted raised center design, two rows of embroidered cutwork lace around neckline, front, hem and sleeves and one row up center back, seamless, gathered front, straight elbow-length sleeves, shoulder pleats, no armhole seams, button and loop closure. Circa 1910.

147. LACE BOLERO JACKET
Short collarless ecru net bolero jacket with hand-appliqued lace all over, short puff sleeves with shirring at cuff, hook and loop closure at neckline. Circa 1930.

Chapter Six

The Flapper and Depression Eras 1920-1935

148. CHIFFON FLAPPER DRESS Sheer peach silk chiffon dress with low waist, wide hip band, bias-cut flared skirt in varying lengths, cloth flowers at hip, scoop neckline, sleeveless. Underslip of pink crepe with peach chiffon lace-trimmed yoke. Circa 1925.

149. EMBROIDERED LACE AND BEADED DRESS
Ecru cotton embroidered lace with gold beading on overdress with surplice bodice with embroidered inset of low squared neckline, beaded waistband, loose front beaded panel with weight at bottom, beading around hem, short demi sleeve with rows of beads connecting sleeve tops, long length, georgette underdress, china silk underslip. Circa 1920.

150. SERGE EGYPTIAN BEADED DRESS

Navy blue wool serge dress with surplice bodice has side belts with bows that snap in back, appliqued lace shawl collar, navy front inset, low waist, two front loose panels with intricate Egyptian patterned beading, side inset pockets with band and bow trim over top. Short sleeves with three cutout sections decorated with bows, side gathered skirt with beaded panels in back. Circa 1920.

151. SEA-GREEN CHIFFON FLAPPER DRESS
Low-waisted silk chiffon dress of sea-green. Scooped neckline, sleeveless, low blouson waist with beaded hip band, lightly gathered skirt with handkerchief panels to add flare, front panels beaded with silver crystal beads and bugle beads over chemise top, four loose beaded panels on skirt, side opening. Circa 1925.

152. BEADED FLAPPER DRESS
Salmon-pink silk georgette dress with deep scooped neckline, front and back panels with higher neckline and "spaghetti strap" cutouts which are heavily beaded with silver and crystal beads and rhinestones, panels beaded in floral and line pattern, beaded low waistline, beaded bands from waist to underarm, double-tiered handkerchief skirt with heavy floral beading pattern, left side snap opening, underchemise of lace-trimmed pink silk. Circa 1925.

153. BEADED SHEATH
Chartreuse silk georgette sheath with scoop neckline, sleeveless, has rhinestone, pearl, crystal and silver beaded patterns from yoke to hem, additional crystal beaded pattern between larger ones, scalloped hemline, green velvet shoulderstraps with rhinestone buckles, green taffeta chemise with adjustable straps, shell-stitched hem, empire waist. Circa 1925.

154. BROCADE DANCING SLIPPERS
Metallic gold brocade shoes with metallic gold leather heels, scalloped leather trim on vamp, cutaway sides, ankle strap closure with pearl button, kidskin lining, leather soles, original label "J & S Slater/New York." Circa 1925.

155. TIERED CHIFFON FLAPPER DRESS
Lemon silk chiffon dress with loose over-bodice with shell, gold, black and amber beading in elliptical pattern over two-tiered gathered skirt of like pattern, scalloped hems, scoop neckline with slight gathering, string bow on shoulder, under-bodice of lace-trimmed chiffon and chiffon underskirt. Circa 1925.

156. FRENCH KIDSKIN T-STRAP SHOES
Gold kidskin shoes with high heels, t-strap construction with petal pattern at ankle and top of shoe, cutaway styling, leather soles, faint original label "Made in Paris especially for O'Connor & Goldberg/Chicago." Worn cloth French Modele Depose labels also inside shoes. Circa 1925.

157. CHIFFON DINNER DRESS
Pale periwinkle-blue silk chiffon dress has surplice bodice with satin stitch embroidery, beading of crystal and silver beads, bodice inset, shirred shoulders, beaded scalloped low waistline, bias-cut tiered flirty skirt, chiffon underskirt with flared hem ruffle, sewn-in chemise of periwinkle silk crepe. Pull-over style. Circa 1925.

158. SEQUIN AND LACE EVENING DRESS
Black sheer net overdress with double layers of net, low-waist, scalloped waist tier over pleated skirt of black silk lace, braid and bead trim on scallops, yoke patterned with black sequins and beads, jet bead "necklace" attached to back neck and hangs over front, scoop neck, sleeveless, wide waist sash of black silk moire with large hip bow, silk crepe chemise with thin straps. Circa 1925.

159. BEADED EVENING GOWN
Black silk chiffon overdress with dense and heavy design of black bugle beads almost completely covering the dress, rounded waist with bias-cut black silk satin beaded hip band, slip-on style with scoop neckline on one side and deep "V" on other to be worn front or back, attached crepe-back satin underdress with chiffon hem band. Circa 1925.

160. SEQUIN AND BEADED SHEATH DRESS
Slip-over sheath dress of two layers of net with iridescent sequins, pink and green beaded rose pattern over entire dress, scoop neckline, sleeveless, high side slits, scalloped sequin and bead design around neckline, beaded scalloped hem, pink tulle underarm insets. Circa 1925.

161. SILVER DANCING SLIPPERS
Silver leather shoes with very high heels, cutout vamp with crisscross design, looped T-strap with ankle buckle, cutaway sides, leather soles, label "Made in Czechoslovakia", original price label from Hudson Bay Co. for $2.95 on heel. Circa 1925.

The Flapper and Depression Eras 1920-1935

162. GEORGETTE FLAPPER DRESS
Deep peach silk georgette dress with scooped "V" neckline trimmed in pearls, rhinestones and crystal beads. Large beaded floral pattern on either side of bodice gathered into low waistline, beaded waistband from side fronts to back, skirt has straight pleated front panel, side and back gathers, two additional horizontal panels of floral and leaf beading, long hanging beaded sash at left waist, shirred shoulders, back similar to front. Circa 1925.

163. GEORGETTE BEADED FLAPPER DRESS
Pale cream silk georgette bias-cut dress in simple lines, center front panel, graceful flared styling, capelet collar, all over beading of crystal bugle beads and embroidery in leaf pattern, scooped neckline, slip-over style. Circa 1925.

164. CHIFFON FLAPPER DRESS
Pumpkin silk chiffon low-waisted dress has rounded neckline, straight loose-fitting bodice with multi-colored Indian bead-type design, bias-cut chiffon skirt with front panel of metallic gold lace with beading, gathered tiered side-to-back overskirt with metallic gold lace and beaded hem bands, sleeveless, pumpkin tulle around neck, chiffon underbodice with thin straps and metallic gold lace trim, silk underskirt. Circa 1925.

165. BEADED SHEATH DRESS
Black dress of woven rayon has net overlay heavily beaded with black bugle beads in pinwheel floral pattern, low squared neckline, left side zipper opening, sleeveless. Age undetermined.

168. SATIN EVENING DRESS
Satin evening dress of rayon floral print with fitted front waist, shirred capelet collar, bias-cut trumpet skirt with two side front seams, seamless back, high curved V-back yoke, self-fabric belt with covered buckle, slip-on style. Circa 1935.

169. SATIN BIAS-CUT EVENING GOWN
Grass-green silk satin has pieced band bodice, draped neckline, band and bow at fitted waist, snug-fitting hip with banded and knotted satin stitched at hips and extending into extremely wide back godets to give fullness to skirt, shorter front, plunging V-back neckline, back skirt panels open from lower torso area to bottom with tacked area at midpoint. Circa 1935.

166. CREPE-BACK SATIN DAY DRESS
Mocha crepe-back silk satin dress has low scarf collar of crepe side of fabric, crepe back yoke, body of dress in satin side, three decorative horizontal tucks at hips in front and back, sharkfin styling at bottom of bodice, bias-cut crepe skirt with self-fabric covered button trim on right side, pointed tab on each side seam at bottom, long straight satin sleeves with crepe sharkfin-style cuffs and button and loop closure. Circa 1925.

166A. CHENILLE CLOCHE HAT
Close-fitting hat of buckram frame and wired brim has crown of woven chenille and braid, brim of blue brocade, mocha silk band, pink and blue ostrich pompom side-trim, black silk lining. Circa 1925.

167. VOILE PEASANT DRESS
Ivory cotton voile peasant dress with smocked neckline, cuffs and low waist, embroidered and fagoted floral pattern on dress front and sleeves, lightly gathered bodice and skirt, couch-stitched neckline and sleeve hems. Circa 1928.

170. GEORGETTE PRINT EVENING DRESS
Black georgette synthetic fabric overdress with splashy floral print is sleeveless with shirred shoulders, surplice empire bodice with gathers, long bias-cut flared skirt, V-shaped back neckline with gathered back bodice, snap side opening, matching bolero jacket with collarless lapels, elbow-length puff sleeve gathered into box-pleated cuff, three shaping darts at back neck, rayon taffeta underslip. Circa 1935.

171. APPLIQUED LACE WEDDING DRESS
Ecru net gown with appliqued lace has bateau neckline, two-layer flared short sleeves, shaped high bustline, fitted waist, bias-cut skirt with upper embroidered hem ruffle and double net bias lower hem ruffle. Multi-layered and ruffled bustle train extends from back waist, left side opening. Circa 1935.

172. GUIPURE LACE EVENING GOWN
Flared sleeveless dress of heavy ecru cotton guipure lace, scooped neckline, sleeveless, separately attached bodice, short guipure jacket with elbow-length trumpet sleeves, satin lining, slip-on style. Circa 1935.

173. THREE COTTON BLOUSES
Three blouses of cotton nainsook have varying necklines and sleeve lengths, all have lace trim, one has bertha collar, fair condition. Circa 1900-1920.

Chapter Seven
The Children's Closet 1850-1920

174. INFANT'S CHRISTENING GOWN
Long white muslin Christening dress with tiny puffed sleeves edged in lingerie lace, lower rounded neckline also edged in lingerie lace and feather-stitching, front bodice of broderie anglaise and tucking, broderie anglaise yoke ruffle extending over sleeve. Long skirt with front panel of rows of tiny tucks between bands of broderie anglaise, tucking and same embroidery at hem, drawstring closures at neck and waist. Circa 1850.

175. WOOL INFANT'S CHRISTENING COAT
Fine cream wool long coat with high yoke, loose yoked capelet collar with feather-stitching around yoke and satin embroidery on gathered cape, slightly gathered straight sleeves edged in featherstitching, two-pearl button yoke with handmade buttonholes, lightly gathered skirt, entire coat lined in cotton. Circa 1900.

176. VELVET AND TAFFETA CHILD'S SUIT
Eggplant velvet with floral stamped design fitted jacket has small standup collar, unusual double cut pointed bodice with inner row of eleven stamped metal buttons and outer row of twelve matching buttons, front darts, princess back with double inverted pleat vent, tight straight sleeves with lace cuff ruffles, skirt of lower velvet front panel, front drape and skirt back of aubergine taffeta, knife-pleated hem ruffle, gathered bustle back, hidden skirt pocket, sateen lining. Circa 1880.

177. COTTON CHILD'S DAY DRESS
Princess-style white muslin dress has front panel of pintucking, Swiss embroidered neck ruffle, bottom of skirt done in alternating panels of horizontal and diagonal pintucking with scalloped hem of Swiss embroidery, corded shoulder seams, lightly gathered sleeves with cuff of diagonal tucks and Swiss embroidery, tucked princess back panel with mother-of-pearl buttons and handmade buttonholes, low waist with gathered back skirt. Circa 1880.

178. SILK CROCHET BABY DRESS
Infant dress of ivory silk crochet with vandyked hem and sleeves, woven blue silk satin ribbon connecting yoke to skirt, blue satin ribbon threaded through collar and back seam.
Circa 1900.

179. TWO INFANT CHRISTENING GOWNS
One cotton gown has Swiss embroidered ribbon on yoke, at yoke edge and down front of dress, ribboned beading around bottom with bands of embroidery and tucking, scalloped edge embroidered hem, drawstring waist and neck, long sleeves. Second gown has tucked front yoke and diagonal tucks alternating with embroidered bands on center front panel, hem ruffle of embroidery, long sleeves with tucked cuffs, open back with button and buttonholes.
Circa 1900.

180. CHILD'S PLEATED DRESS
Small child's dress of white batiste with bertha collar trimmed in mechlin lace, front panel of alternating bands of lace insertion with box-pleated batiste, lace and batiste lower pockets, double row of lace hem, back bodice similar to front, center opening

with covered buttons and hidden placket, hip-length band of lace with lower skirt of inverted box pleats, straight sleeves with insertion trim and lace cuff ruffles. Circa 1900.

181. CHILD'S COTTON LOW-WAISTED DRESS

Child's dress of white cotton batiste with squared neckline trimmed in guipure lace, center front panel of tiny pintucks with lace down center, bretelles with guipure and Valenciennes lace edge ruffles, beading around low waist, gathered skirt with embroidered band and hem, short puffed sleeves with lace cuff and ruffle, back hidden placket with buttons. Circa 1900.

182. CHILD'S BLOUSON DRESS

White muslin dress with blouson bodice, bertha collar with ribboned beading and lace edging, pleated yoke with beading, lace neck ruffle, gathered skirt, long gathered sleeves with lace edging, button and handmade buttonhole closure on back pleated yoke, stiff cotton bodice interlining. Circa 1910.

183. BOY'S PIQUE COAT
Small boy's coat of white pique with embroidered sailor collar, double-breasted front, two front box pleats, hip belt threaded through pleats, one back box pleat, straight long sleeves with scalloped cuff. Circa 1910.

184. PIQUE GIRL'S COAT AND HAT
Small girl's coat of white pique with knife-pleated front and back, wide embroidered pointed collar, embroidered hem and cuffs, gathered sleeves pleated into cuffs, button and loop closure, wide-brim hat of pique of embroidered circle with buttonholes which buttons onto wide circular embroidered brim, grosgrain ties. Circa 1910.

185. CHILD'S DRESS OF EYELET EMBROIDERY
Small child's dress with one-piece high yoke and sleeves of white eyelet embroidery, square neckline, guipure trim on neckline and sleeves, gathered skirt with scalloped edge of eyelet, Valenciennes trim at waist, snap closure at back. Circa 1912.

186. MIXED LOT OF CHILDREN'S WHITEWEAR
Consists of child's short cotton jacket with Swiss embroidery and ruched panels and neck ruffle, three half slips of varying sizes with tucking, Swiss embroidery, lace and Cluny lace, varying eras.

Chapter Eight
Boots to Bonnets

187. FRENCH BLACK LEATHER THREE-STRAP SHOES
Black kidskin leather shoes with pointed toes, spool heels, three separate straps with shoe buttons, silver bead trim on vamp and straps, leather soles, kidskin lining, faint French label on lining. Circa 1915.

188. SUEDE PUMPS
Grey suede pumps with spool heels, high vamp decorated with silver beading and beaded bow, leather soles, suede lining, slightly-pointed toes, original label "H. Jantzens Shoe Co./NY." Circa 1910.

189. ONE-STRAP SUEDE PUMPS
Pair of gray suede pumps with low spool heels, high squared vamp, wide ankle strap with decorative metal shoe button, leather soles, kidskin lining, pointed toes, no label. Circa 1918.

190. FRENCH THREE-STRAP BEADED LEATHER SHOES
Kid leather pumps of olive black with low spool heels of black leather, three straps with shoe buttons, rounded vamp and toe, black beaded design on vamp and straps, kid lining, French inner label, original label "B. Altman & Co./Paris-New York." Circa 1890.

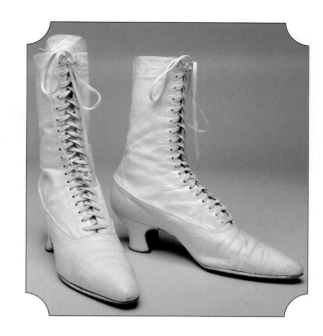

191. SUEDE HIGH TOP SHOES
Brown suede high-topped shoes have very pointed toes, buttonhole grommets, cotton laces, spool heels, leather soles, stitched and nailed, canvas lining, original label "Diamond Shoe & Garment Co./Charleston, W. VA." Also, canvas stamp "155 51058/Boyd-Welsh Process/845." Circa 1912.

192. KIDSKIN HIGH TOP SHOES
White kidskin high-topped shoes have pointed toes, perforated vamp, grommets, cotton laces, low chunky spool heels, leather soles, canvas lining, label in one "Laird, Scholer and Co./Milady" and in other "Wetherby Kayser Shoes/Los Angeles, California." Circa 1910.

193. KIDSKIN HIGH TOP SHOES WITH SCALLOPS
Camel kidskin leather shoes have scalloped tops, medium spool heels with metal trim, grommets and cotton laces, perforated vamp seam, canvas lining, leather soles, no label. Circa 1915.

194. LEATHER HIGH TOP SHOES WITH BUTTERFLY DECORATION
Black leather shoes with high scalloped tops, buttonholes, brown grosgrain laces, pointed toes with brown and gold beaded butterfly design on vamps and beaded leaf design along lacing holes, spool heels, leather soles, canvas lining. Original label "Dunne's Shoe Store/Stockton, Cal." Circa 1915.

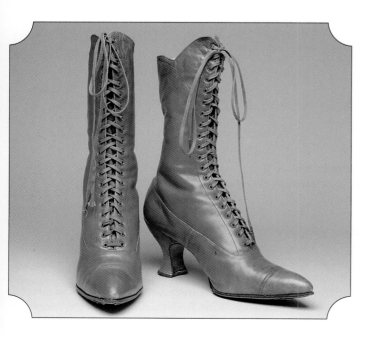

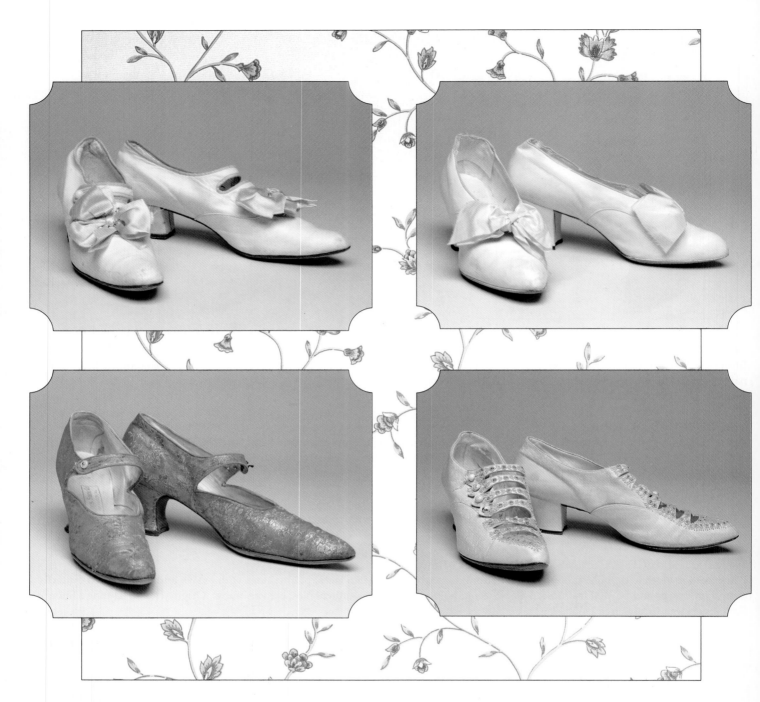

195. WHITE KID PUMPS
White kid pumps have chunky heel, semi-rounded toe, one grommet lacing tied with ivory silk bow, kidskin lining, leather sole, original label "Dee-Standard Shoe Co./Ogden, Utah." Circa 1918.

196. THREE-STRAP KID PUMPS
Ivory kidskin pumps with short chunky heels have three straps with shoe buttons, bottom strap has ecru silk double bow, slightly squared toe, bias edging in ecru, leather soles, kidskin lining, original label "Herman F. Heckert/Appleton, Wis." Circa 1880.

197. BROCADE DANCING SHOES
Silver brocade shoes with extremely pointed toes, spool heels, ankle strap with shoe buttons, leather soles, kidskin lining. Original label "Innes Shoe Co./Los Angeles, Cal." Circa 1918.

198. BEADED LEATHER STRAP SHOES
Ivory leather pumps with low chunky heel have cutout strap design with four shoe buttons, two cutouts on vamp, vamp and straps beaded with blue and pearl beads, kidskin lining, leather soles, worn sewn-in original label "Trust Trademark/Made in USA Soro..." (Company name worn.) Circa 1880.

Chapter Eight

199. LEATHER OXFORDS
Rust-brown leather oxfords have stacked wooden spool heels, metal grommets, cord lacings, leather soles, kidskin and canvas lining, original label too worn to read. Circa 1900.

200. LEATHER OXFORDS BY RED CROSS
Dark camel oxford-styled shoes have stitched vamp, perforated upper vamp, metal grommets, flat cotton laces, wooden chunky heels, leather soles, kidskin lining. Inner label "Hedberg Bros./Tacoma, WA." Embossed on sole "Krohn-Fecheimer & Co./Cinti, USA/Red Cross Noiseless Shoe/Special." Circa 1910.

201. QUILTED WEDGIE-STYLE BOOT
Black velveteen boots have wedge-type heel, genuine fur trim, velvet tongue, three ribbon ties, quilted inner lining, leather soles, no label. Circa 1880.

202. ENGLISH PLUSH HAT WITH BIRD MEDALLION

Royal blue plush molded buckram frame hat has flattened rounded crown, short flat brim, two bands of metallic gold ribbon, rosette of several layers of metallic gold fabric and blue velvet ribbon; in center a molded bird head with glass eyes and partial body, black silk lining, original label "Derniere Mode Et Premiere Qualite/Tailored Hats/Phipps/London Paris/Berlin New York/Registered No.29317." Circa 1915.

203. PANAMA HAT WITH CHERRY TRIM

White Panama straw hat has floppy brim, one upturned side, domed crown, striped silk ribbon band and bow with wide moire silk double bow trimmed with large bunch of paper mache cherries, silk lining. Circa 1900.

204. PANAMA HAT WITH FLOWER TRIM

White panama straw hat has flattened crown, wide slightly turned up brim, black and ivory checked silk taffeta band and bow with three black cloth floral and grass decorations, velvet inner band, silk lining. Circa 1900.

205. STRAW PANSY HAT

Plum-colored straw hat with rounded crown and narrow brim on one side and wide upturned brim with velvet pansy bunches, gathered green grosgrain ribbon band with smaller pansy bunches as trim, velvet inner brim, black silk lining. Circa 1890.

206. BLACK PLUSH HAT
Molded black plush felt hat has high rounded crown, small turned up brim on one side and very wide turned up brim (which is again turned down on edge) on other side trimmed with black velvet bows, black and white ostrich pompoms and plumes, black silk lining. Circa 1910.

207. BLACK PLUSH HAT WITH JEWELED TRIM
Molded black plush felt hat is more compact version of previous lot with derby crown trimmed with brown ombre ostrich plume and gold metallic and velvet ribbon, gold filigree setting inset with large faux topaz, buckram inner brim, black silk lining. Circa 1900.

208. PLUSH HAT WITH ROSE AND OSTRICH TRIM
Brown taupe plush hat with molded buckram frame has derby crown, slightly turned up short brim on one side and wide turned up brim on other side, printed silk bow covered with large bunch of pink cloth roses and two pink to brown ombre ostrich plumes, black plush underbrim, black silk lining. Circa 1900.

209. LADIES MARQUIS HAT
Black molded velvet brim in tricorner style, molded buckram flattened crown covered in black satin with gathered band, large tulip-shaped beaded jewel covering tuft of black and white quill feathers, bias satin edging on brim, silk lining. Circa 1913.

210. STRAW HAT WITH OSTRICH PLUME
Navy blue fine straw hat with wider turned up brim on one side, rounded crown, wide blue patterned silk ribbon band, navy and blue ombre ostrich plumes as trim, black sateen lining. Circa 1912.

211. STRAW TOCQUE
Tiny black hat of fine straw crown and rough, heavy straw brim with upturned sides, black sequin trim on brim edge, gathered organza covering crown sides, large black cloth flower on side, bunch of small flowers tacked at back and underbrim, sateen lining. Circa 1890.

212. VELVET AND FUR HAT
Black velvet hat with soft, flattened crown covered with iridescent blue round and bugle beads in sun designs, molded buckram upturned brim lined with soft black fur, silk lining. Circa 1917.

213. FUR AND VELVETEEN HAT WITH FLOWERS
Wine-colored velveteen hat with oval crown, molded buckram and wired frame, standup brim covered with black fur and large fuchsia and pink flowers, velvet back inner band, ivory silk lining, original label "Kurzman/Fifth Avenue/Thirty Sixth St./New York." Circa 1912.

214. BLACK NEAPOLITAN BONNET
Wired-frame bonnet with black horsehair ruffles comprising body, left side upturned with horsehair bow, black sequin trim on bow, black satin ribbon intertwined with ruffles, large bunch of white cloth lilacs on top, black sateen lining. Circa 1890.

215. NEAPOLITAN BONNET WITH FLORAL TRIM
Natural colored horsehair straw bonnet with wired brim under rows of ruffled and swirled horsehair, upturned brim on one side, black velvet bow with ivory tulle at brim, garland of johnny jump-ups on brim, small bunch on underbrim with velvet bow, ivory silk lining. Circa 1903.

216. WIRED-BRIM NEAPOLITAN BONNET
Black horsehair bonnet with wired frame, flat crown, medium shaped brim with trim of veiling, black cloth flowers in back, black cloth flowers with gray forget-me-nots in front, pleated and gathered organza on underbrim, sateen lining, velveteen inner brim lining. Circa 1900.

217. HORSEHAIR MOURNING CAP
Black horsehair mourning cap of several rosettes of horsehair, crinoline base, black velvet ties. Circa 1890.

218. HORSEHAIR PICTURE HAT
Finely woven apricot horsehair in molded shell-type pattern, rounded crown, wide floppy brim with small wire around edge, large apricot cloth rose with leaves, grosgrain inner band, original label "Cirin's/Pasadena." Circa 1930.

219. WOVEN GRASS TURBAN
Woven blue and red striped grass is interwoven into high-crowned turban style with wired brim, unique stand-up pleating from crown to brim, large blue velvet bows in front, small turned up brim with blue velvet underbrim and inner brim, sateen lining. Circa 1900.

220. STRAW HAT WITH FLOWERS
Large navy blue straw hat with flat brim and wide, slightly turned-up brim has blue ombre braid on brim and under brim and garland of roses, morning glories and orange blossoms over a gathered silk ribbon, black silk lining. Circa 1910.

221. STRAW BONNET WITH SILK ROSES
Natural straw bonnet with slightly flattened rounded crown and wide flat brim is trimmed with peach velvet ribbon covered in the front with peach silk roses and smaller flowers, raffia trim on edge. Circa 1930.

222. FUR TURBAN
Large molded buckram and wired frame turban shape is covered with dark brown fur, closely upturned brim with burgundy velvet ribbon and woven braid with two mink heads as trim, silk lining. Circa 1910.

222A. FUR MUFF
Large black fur muff with guard hairs still remaining, lining missing, cotton batting interlining. Circa 1910.

223. GAINSBOROUGH HAT
Black velvet wide-brimmed hat turned up on one side, covered with black and deep pink striped silk ribbon, curled black and pink ombre ostrich plumes, large rose, oval crown, velvet under and inner brims, silk lining, molded buckram frame. Circa 1890.

224. MEN'S BEAVER TOP HAT WITH ORIGINAL CARRYING CASE
Black beaver top hat with non-collapsible crown, felt band, leather inner band, satin lining, original label "Desmond's/Los Angeles." Heavy tan leather carrying case with red leather inner case form for hat lined with gathered burgundy silk with lift-up handles, separate red leather piece lined in silk to set over the hat for additional protection with buckles to attach to case, fitted tan leather top with carrying handle, front lock on case. Circa 1850.

225. MEN'S WOOL FELT TOP HAT IN HATBOX
Gray wool felt top hat with black felt band, silk grosgrain edging, leather inner band, corded drawstring in back for fitting, satin lining, original label "Lock & Co./Hatters/St. James Street/London." Cardboard hat box with inner frame for high-crowned hat of gold cardboard with eagle motif from Knox of New York. Circa 1900.

226. MEN'S BROWN FELT DERBY
Brown wool felt derby has round crown, grosgrain ribbon band with bow, slight upturned brim on sides, grosgrain edging, leather inner band embossed "Eastside", gold label stamp "Milwaukee/Pantke-Harpke Co./390 S. Bowter St." Circa 1900.

227. MEN'S STRAW BOATER
Natural straw hat with flat oval crown and flat brim, hatband of black and brown-striped grosgrain silk, remains of inner band lining, label "The Rossley Hat." Circa 1912.

228. WIDE-BRIMMED STRAW HAT
Large hat of natural straw with flat crown, wide brim, cloth roses trim, leather inner band, remains of paper lining. Circa 1910.

229. UNTRIMMED PLUSH FELT HAT
A wide brim slightly turned up, flat-crowned hat of white beaver plush felt with stiffened velveteen inner band, paper label from Hewlett Robin Co. New York. Trims were removed from hat in the past. Circa 1900.

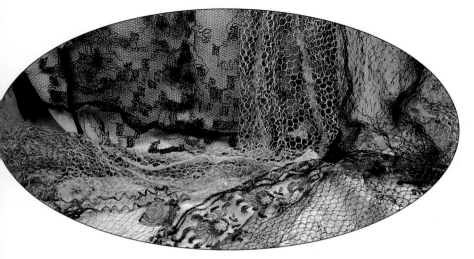

230A. LOT OF OSTRICH PLUMES
Lot of seventeen early ostrich plumes of various colors including three ombre ones.

230B. LOT OF OSTRICH PLUMES
Lot of sixteen early ostrich plumes of various colors and one pheasant fluff with tail feathers.

231. LOT OF HAT VEILING
Lot of seven pieces of veiling, some silk, in browns and blacks, in various sizes.

Bibliography and Books of Interest

Blum, Stella. Everyday Fashions of the Twenties as Pictured in Sears and other Catalogs. Dover Publications, Inc. New York. 1981.

Bradfield, Nancy. Costume in Detail 1730-1930. Plays, Inc. Boston, Massachusetts. 1968.

Cartledge, Pamela. Dress for All Occasions: Women's Costumes from the 1880's and 1890's. The Connecticut Historical Society. The Bond Press, Inc. Hartford, Connecticut. 1987.

Dolan, Maryanne. Vintage Clothing 1880-1980 Third Edition. Books Americana. Florence, Alabama. 1995.

Ettinger, Roseann. Handbags. Schiffer Publishing, Ltd. West Chester, Pennsylvania. 1991.

Ewing, Elizabeth. Dress and Undress A History of Women's Underwear. B.T. Batsford Ltd. London, England. 1989.

Gerson, Roselyn. Vintage Vanity Bags and Purses. Collector Books. Paducah, Kentucky. 1994.

Haertig, Evelyn. More Beautiful Purses. Gallery Graphics Press. Carmel, California. 1990.

Hall, Carrie A. From Hoopskirts to Nudity. The Caxton Printers, Ltd. Caldwell, Idaho. 1946.

Kurella, Elizabeth M. The Secrets of Real Lace. The Printmill. Kalamazoo, Michigan. 1994.

Picken, Mary Brooks. The Fashion Dictionary. Funk & Wagnalls. New York, New York. 1957.

Theriault, Florence. In Their Fashion. Doll Costumes and Accessories, 1850-1925. Gold Horse Publishing. Annapolis, Maryland. 1994.

Theriault, Florence. The Way They Wore. Doll Costumes and Accessories, 1850-1925. Gold Horse Publishing. Annapolis, Maryland. 1993.

Ulseth, Hazel and Shannon, Helen. Antique Children's Fashions 1880-1900. Hobby House Press. Cumberland, Maryland. 1982.

Ulseth, Hazel and Shannon, Helen. Victorian Fashions. Volume I 1880-1890. Hobby House Press, Cumberland, Maryland. 1988.

Ulseth, Hazel and Shannon, Helen. Victorian Fashions. Volume II 1890-1905. Hobby House Press. Cumberland, Maryland. 1989.

Waugh, Norah. The Cut of Women's Clothes 1600-1930. Theatre Arts Books. New York, New York. 1968.

Wilcox, R. Turner. The Dictionary of Costume. Charles Scribner's Sons. New York, New York. 1969.

Index

Blouses . . . . .pp. 11, 18, 22, 24-26, 52, 53, 88

Children's Clothing . . . . .pp. 42, 90, 91, 92,9 3, 94, 95

Coats and Jackets . . . . .pp. 9, 11, 18, 20, 25, 26, 27, 48-52, 53, 67-70

Collars . . . . .pp. 27

Corsets . . . . .pp. 30, 31

Dresses . . . . .pp. 7, 10, 12, 20, 22-24, 33, 36, 38-43, 71-86

Evening Gowns . . . . .pp. 6, 8, 9, 13-16, 19, 21, 34, 35, 37, 86, 86-89

Fans . . . . .pp. 67

Gloves . . . . .pp. 60-62

Hats . . . . .pp. 7, 16, 18, 19, 22, 23, 33, 34, 39, 44-46, 48, 86, 100-109

Lingerie . . . . .pp. 28, 29, 31, 32

Men's Clothing . . . . .pp. 20, 27

Parasols . . . . .pp. 20, 63-66

Purses . . . . .pp. 19, 24, 25, 33-35, 45-47, 54-59

Shoes . . . . .pp. 5, 7, 13, 44, 46, 76, 77, 81, 96-99

Skirts . . . . .pp. 18, 22, 25, 26

Suits . . . . .pp. 16, 17, 19, 21, 44-47